WHY DIDN'T THEY TEACH ME THIS IN SCHOOL?

99 PERSONAL
MONEY MANAGEMENT
PRINCIPLES TO LIVE BY

WORKBOOK

55 EXERCISES TO REINFORCE YOUR MONEY MANAGEMENT SKILLS

CARY SIEGEL

Information provided is from the author's perspective. The author takes no responsibility for the reader's financial success or failure.

No part of this book may be reproduced or transmitted in any form or by any means—except by a reviewer who may quote passages in a review—without permission from the author. For more information, please contact carysiegel@yahoo.com.

ISBN-10: 1543294375
ISBN-13: 9781543294378
Library of Congress Control Number: 2017903016
CreateSpace Independent Publishing Platform
North Charleston, South Carolina

Praise for *Why Didn't They Teach Me This in School?*
99 Personal Money Management Principles to Live By

"As the name implies, this book is about all of the basic personal finance lessons that they probably should've taught us in school and didn't. There are 99 tips, tricks, and lessons for personal finance that pretty much everyone should know and reviewers have called it 'a great gift idea for high school and college graduates.' We happen to agree."

Life Hack
10 personal finance books you need to read

"While some of the lessons seem unorthodox, they are easy to remember and thought provoking. This book is an easily digestible read, offering vast amounts of practical advice."

eBay
Top 5 books to help keep you financially responsible

"Believe me, Cary Siegel knows what he's talking about, and turns money talk into an understandable and easy topic."

Bustle
Top 6 books on how to be an adult that every
twentysomething needs to know

"This book breaks down what we should've learned about managing our money growing up."

Elitedaily.com
16 money books Gen-Yers must read

Another Gift to My Children

Sam, Sabrina, Julia, Jack, and Luke: Keep exercising both your mind and body. I promise you that it will pay off.

Caveat to All

This book is intended to be a companion book to "Why Didn't They Teach Me This in School? 99 Personal Money Management Principles to Live By". **This is the only time you will probably ever hear this from an author—please don't purchase this workbook unless you have already read the book.**

CONTENTS

FOREWORD

Since my book *Why Didn't They Teach Me This in School? 99 Personal Money Management Principles to Live By* was published, I've been asked by professors, teachers, parents, and students to develop learning activities that reinforce the principles in my book. So I finally sat down and did just that.

The exercises in this workbook were personally developed to cause the next step of thinking for students and young adults (and older adults) to make sound personal financial decisions in their everyday lives. My hope is that this workbook causes individuals to ask even more questions regarding money management.

The workbook can be used for written assignments, discussions, or personal thoughts. It can also be used for assignments in a yearlong or semester course (as many professors and teachers have done). Please use the workbook in whatever format that makes sense to you. Becoming more financially literate is the ultimate goal!

LIFE
LESSON

PRINCIPLE 1:
MARRY THE "FINANCIALLY RIGHT" PERSON

EXERCISE 1:

Write about/discuss your "money philosophy." Are you a saver or a spender? If someone gave you $10,000 to spend on whatever you want, what would you do with it?

Notes

PRINCIPLE 2:

STAY MARRIED TO THE "FINANCIALLY RIGHT" PERSON

EXERCISE 2:

Describe your perfect partner—not just in terms of money but also in terms of other attributes.

Notes

PRINCIPLE 3:
HAVING AND RAISING CHILDREN COSTS LOTS OF MONEY

EXERCISE 3:

Use the Internet and any other resources to break down the cost of raising a child from infancy through high school. Some costs you need to include are food, clothing, shelter, childcare, health care, education, entertainment, sports, and other extracurricular activities. Bonus exercise: What are the four-year tuition, room, board, and other expenses to attend the best state university in your state? And what are the same expenses for the best private university in your state?

Notes

_____

_____

_____

_____

_____

_____

_____

_____

_____

_____

_____

_____

_____

_____

_____

_____

_____

_____

_____

_____

_____

_____

_____

_____

_____

_____

_____

_____

PRINCIPLE 4:
ALWAYS LIVE BELOW YOUR MEANS

EXERCISE 4:

Identify a professional athlete or entertainer who went bankrupt. Write about/discuss how it happened.

Notes

_____

_____

_____

_____

_____

_____

_____

_____

_____

_____

_____

_____

_____

_____

_____

_____

_____

_____

_____

_____

_____

_____

_____

_____

_____

PRINCIPLE 5:
TAKE CARE OF YOUR "STUFF"

EXERCISE 5:

Write down the top five most expensive things that you own. How much would it cost to replace each of them? Be honest—have you taken good care of them, and has the value increased, stayed the same, or declined because of how you took care of them?

Notes

PRINCIPLE 6:

EXPAND YOUR CIRCLE OF FRIENDS/ASSOCIATES, AND KEEP IN TOUCH WITH THEM

EXERCISE 6:

This is a fun one. List five of your friends, and predict what their careers will be. Discuss how you may benefit from maintaining a relationship with them.

Notes

PRINCIPLE 7:

YOU TAKE AWAY MORE FROM YOUR FIRST COUPLE OF JOBS THAN YOU GIVE

EXERCISE 7:

If you have worked, write down/discuss three things you've learned from your job. If you haven't worked, do the same for an activity you have participated in.

Notes

Exercise 8

PRINCIPLE 8:

SPEND JUST ONE HOUR EACH WEEK LEARNING ABOUT PERSONAL FINANCE

EXERCISE 8:

Interview a person you believe has done well managing his or her money. Write about/discuss what you learned from that person.

Notes

PRINCIPLE 9:
GET RICH SLOWLY

EXERCISE 9:

There are numerous examples and articles on people getting rich slowly. Write a one-page summary of an example or article about "getting rich slowly."

Notes

PRINCIPLE 10:

SET (REALISTIC) SHORT-TERM FINANCIAL GOALS

EXERCISE 10:

Set three monthly financial goals and three financial goals for this year.

Notes

PRINCIPLE 11:

SET (REALISTIC) LONG-TERM FINANCIAL GOALS

EXERCISE 11:

Set five ten-year financial goals.

Notes

_____
_____
_____
_____
_____
_____
_____
_____
_____
_____
_____
_____
_____
_____
_____
_____
_____
_____
_____
_____
_____
_____
_____
_____
_____
_____
_____
_____

PRINCIPLE 12:
ALWAYS KNOW THE SCORE— YOUR NET WORTH

EXERCISE 12:

Use the net worth statement from principle 12 in *"Why Didn't They Teach Me This in School?"* to determine your net worth. Show your work.

Notes

_____

_____

_____

_____

_____

_____

_____

_____

_____

_____

_____

_____

_____

_____

_____

_____

_____

_____

_____

_____

_____

_____

_____

_____

_____

Budgeting and Saving Lesson

PRINCIPLE 13:

DEVELOP A WRITTEN BUDGET, AND EVALUATE IT EVERY SINGLE MONTH

EXERCISE 13:

Use the budgeting worksheet from principle 13 in *"Why Didn't They Teach Me This in School?"* to develop a monthly budget. What is your total budget? Where is most of your money going? What surprised you about your budget? Write about/discuss your answers.

Notes

PRINCIPLE 14:
GIVE YOURSELF AN ANNUAL FINANCIAL PHYSICAL

EXERCISE 14:

Ask your parents if they do this. Also, ask if they know their net worth. Lastly, ask them if they have a written monthly budget. Write about/discuss your findings.

Notes

_____
_____
_____
_____
_____
_____
_____
_____
_____
_____
_____
_____
_____
_____
_____
_____
_____
_____
_____
_____
_____
_____
_____
_____
_____
_____
_____

PRINCIPLES 15 AND 16:

SAVE/INVEST 50 PERCENT OF EVERY SALARY INCREASE; SAVE 90 PERCENT OF EVERY BONUS (OR NON-PLANNED INCOME)

EXERCISE 15:

Since this was the most important lesson I learned from a teacher/professor in my nineteen years of schooling, I ask that you do the same. Write about/discuss the most important lesson you have learned from a teacher/professor.

Notes

_____

_____

_____

_____

_____

_____

_____

_____

_____

_____

_____

_____

_____

_____

_____

_____

_____

_____

_____

_____

_____

_____

_____

_____

_____

_____

_____

PRINCIPLE 17:

UNDERSTAND YOUR EMPLOYEE BENEFITS; THEY ARE WORTH SIGNIFICANT DOLLARS

EXERCISE 16:

Ask a family member to go over his or her employee benefits. List and explain them.

Notes

PRINCIPLE 18:
ALWAYS HAVE AN EMERGENCY FUND

EXERCISE 17:

Describe an instance when you wished you had money to do something special. How much was needed? How would you go about planning for that now?

Notes

PRINCIPLE 19:
HAVE AN EMERGENCY MONTH EVERY JANUARY

EXERCISE 18:

Pretend next month is an emergency month. What spending habits would you change to save money? What spending habits would you ask your family to change? How would these changes affect your life? Approximately how much money would you and your family save? Write about/discuss your answers.

Notes

PRINCIPLES 20-22:

COUPONS MAKE SENSE; SHOP AROUND FOR DISCOUNTS; MAIL IN YOUR REBATE OFFERS

EXERCISE 19:

During a week-long period, look for coupons, discounts, and rebates offered in the paper (particularly on Sunday), through direct mail, and on the Internet for products you or your family uses. Calculate how much money would be saved by using these offers. Cut out and print the coupons, discounts, and rebates you found.

Notes

_____
_____
_____
_____
_____
_____
_____
_____
_____
_____
_____
_____
_____
_____
_____
_____
_____
_____
_____
_____
_____
_____
_____
_____
_____
_____
_____

PRINCIPLE 23:

HAVE A SAVING VERSUS A SPENDING MIND-SET

EXERCISE 20:

Identify (anonymously) one "saver" and one "spender," and write about/discuss the differences in their behavior.

Notes

Spending Lesson

PRINCIPLE 24:

DON'T TRY TO KEEP UP WITH THE JONESES; THEY'RE GOING BANKRUPT

EXERCISE 21:

The concept behind this principle is that adults feel peer pressure just like high school and college students do. Write about/discuss a time when you felt peer pressure and how you positively or negatively dealt with it.

Notes

_____
_____
_____
_____
_____
_____
_____
_____
_____
_____
_____
_____
_____
_____
_____
_____
_____
_____
_____
_____
_____
_____
_____
_____
_____
_____

PRINCIPLE 25:

DON'T UNDERESTIMATE THE COST OF OWNERSHIP

EXERCISE 22:

If you live in a house, list the specific monthly costs associated with owning the home (you will need your parents' help on this one). Bonus exercise: If you have a car, list the specific costs of owning the car over the past year.

Notes

PRINCIPLES 26, 29, AND 30:

PRIORITIZE YOUR SPENDING; DETERMINE WHAT EVERYDAY PRODUCTS AND SERVICES ARE IMPORTANT TO YOU; MAKE SURE THE LUXURIES YOU AFFORD YOURSELF ARE TRULY IMPORTANT TO YOU

EXERCISE 23:

Put together a priority list of your needs (housing, clothes, food, transportation, etc.). Then put together a priority list of your wants (things that aren't necessary). Write about/discuss your top-ranked need and want. Do the same for your lowest-ranked need and want.

Notes

_____

_____

_____

_____

_____

_____

_____

_____

_____

_____

_____

_____

_____

_____

_____

_____

_____

_____

_____

_____

_____

_____

_____

_____

_____

PRINCIPLES 27 AND 28:

STAY AWAY FROM "GREAT DEALS" AND "SMALL BARGAINS" THAT REALLY AREN'T

EXERCISE 24:

The book talks about several specific "great deals" and "small bargains" that aren't. Write about/discuss one (not mentioned in the book) that you've heard of or actually happened to you.

Notes

PRINCIPLE 31:

BEFORE YOU BUY ANYTHING EXPENSIVE, STOP AND THINK ABOUT WHETHER YOU NEED IT

EXERCISE 25:

What products do you consider expensive? How much does something have to cost to be considered expensive? Write about/discuss your answers.

Notes

PRINCIPLE 32:
DROP "UNHEALTHY" SPENDING HABITS

EXERCISE 26:

Identify and calculate the annual cost of one "unhealthy" spending habit. Since cigarette smoking was an example in the book, please use another habit.

Notes

PRINCIPLE 33:

KNOW WHAT YOUR MONTHLY BILLS ARE AND TAKE ACTION WHEN THEY ARE INCREASED

EXERCISE 27:

Without allowing them to look up their payments, ask your parents what their last month's bill was for the following items: cable, Internet, cell phone, electric, gas, and water. Now have them look up their actual payments. Check and see how close they were on each expense. Write about/discuss your findings.

Notes

_____

_____

_____

_____

_____

_____

_____

_____

_____

_____

_____

_____

_____

_____

_____

_____

_____

_____

_____

_____

_____

_____

_____

_____

_____

PRINCIPLES 34 AND 35:

PAY ALL YOUR BILLS ON TIME EVERY SINGLE MONTH INCLUDING THE GOVERNMENT

EXERCISE 28:

How much are the fees (and what are other potential consequences) for being late in paying each of the following expenses—IRS taxes, local parking ticket, and cell-phone and electric bills?

Notes

PRINCIPLE 36:

IT'S OK TO OVERPAY THE
IRS (BY A LITTLE) OVER THE
COURSE OF A YEAR

EXERCISE 29:

Ask five people who have paid taxes for the past several years if they ever received a tax refund. If they did, ask them what they did with their refund money. Write about/discuss your findings.

Notes

PRINCIPLE 37:

CHECK EVERY BILL YOU GET, ESPECIALLY THOSE FOR HEALTH CARE

EXERCISE 30:

Ask your parents to share their health-care plan with you. What is their monthly premium? And what is the definition of a monthly premium? What is their annual deductible? And what is the definition of a "deductible"? Bonus exercise: Look at the last doctor bill you had, and see how much was charged by the doctor and how much you paid (they are usually different). Write about/discuss your findings.

Notes

_____

_____

_____

_____

_____

_____

_____

_____

_____

_____

_____

_____

_____

_____

_____

_____

_____

_____

_____

_____

_____

_____

_____

_____

_____

PRINCIPLE 38:
REVIEW AND KEEP ALL YOUR RECEIPTS

EXERCISE 31:

For one month keep all your receipts. At the end of the month, log all your receipts in categories that make sense for you. Report on how much was spent in each category. If needed, you can shorten the time frame to one week.

Notes

PRINCIPLE 39:
BUY A CAR THAT FITS IN YOUR CURRENT BUDGET

EXERCISE 32:

Pretend you have $25,000 to purchase a car (including tax). Use the Internet and classified ads to determine a specific car to purchase. What specific car would you purchase? Why would you purchase the car? Report on what car you purchased, including make, model, year, and any other specifics.

Notes

PRINCIPLE 40:

PURCHASE LAST YEAR'S MODEL ON HIGH-TICKET ITEMS

EXERCISE 33:

Use kbb.com to compare the price of the car you decided to purchase if it were brand new, one year old with ten thousand miles on it, three years old with thirty-five thousand miles on it, and five years old with seventy-five thousand miles on it. Which one makes the most sense to buy, and why?

Notes

PRINCIPLE 41:
NEGOTIATE EVERYTHING

EXERCISE 34:

Describe a situation where you negotiated a better outcome for yourself. Or describe a situation where you would have had a better outcome if you had used some basic negotiation skills.

Notes

PRINCIPLE 42:
SPEND NOW TO SAVE LATER

EXERCISE 35:

The book discusses several "spend now to save later" examples. Write about/discuss an example not discussed in the book.

Notes

Debt and Credit Card Lesson

PRINCIPLES 43 AND 44:
DEBT IS BAD; IF YOU ARE IN DEBT, GET OUT OF IT QUICKLY

EXERCISE 36:

Go to usdebtclock.org, and record the following information: (1) US national debt, (2) student loan debt, and (3) credit card debt. Approximately how much does each of these increase in one minute? Please note the date and time of your recording. What is your reaction to what you see?

Notes

_____

_____

_____

_____

_____

_____

_____

_____

_____

_____

_____

_____

_____

_____

_____

_____

_____

_____

_____

_____

_____

_____

_____

_____

_____

_____

PRINCIPLES 45 AND 46:

DO NOT GET A CREDIT CARD IN COLLEGE; AFTER COLLEGE HAVE ONLY ONE CREDIT CARD

EXERCISE 37:

Conduct a survey of three students and three non-students. Ask each person (1) how many credit cards he or she has and (2) if he or she has more than one, what is the purpose of each one. Report your findings.

Notes

_____

_____

_____

_____

_____

_____

_____

_____

_____

_____

_____

_____

_____

_____

_____

_____

_____

_____

_____

_____

_____

_____

_____

_____

_____

_____

PRINCIPLE 47:

IF YOU HAVE TO HAVE ONE CREDIT CARD, PAY THE BALANCE EVERY MONTH

EXERCISE 38:

Answer the following questions and discuss: (1) What percentage of American households have credit-card debt? (2) What is the average debt each of these households have? (3) What percentage of graduating college seniors have credit-card debt? (4) What is the average credit-card debt for these graduating seniors?

Notes

PRINCIPLES 48 AND 49:

DEVELOP AND MAINTAIN A GOOD CREDIT CARD RATING AND FICO SCORE

EXERCISE 39:

Write about/discuss three things you are going to do in the future to develop a good FICO score.

Notes

_____
_____
_____
_____
_____
_____
_____
_____
_____
_____
_____
_____
_____
_____
_____
_____
_____
_____
_____
_____
_____
_____
_____
_____
_____
_____
_____

PRINCIPLE 50:
UNDERSTAND THE TIME VALUE OF MONEY

EXERCISE 40:

Answer this question: Why is it important to understand the time value of money?

Notes

Investing
Lesson

PRINCIPLE 51:
MANAGE YOUR OWN MONEY

EXERCISE 41:

Compare at least two of the top ten online brokers in regard to quality, services, and price. Which one would you use, and why?

Notes

PRINCIPLE 52:
DON'T FALL FOR "GET RICH QUICK" SCHEMES

EXERCISE 42:

Write about/discuss a "get rich quick" scheme that has been tried on you, a friend, or a family member.

Notes

PRINCIPLES 53 AND 55:

DON'T LOOK FOR THE FINANCIAL HOME RUN; SINGLES AND DOUBLES RESULT IN THE LONG-TERM WIN; DON'T PLAY HUNCHES IN THE STOCK MARKET, AND DON'T INVEST IN A FRIEND'S "CAN'T MISS" TIP

EXERCISE 43:

For every Google, there is an Ask Jeeves (one of the first search engines and a "can't miss stock"). Identify a similar comparison in another industry, and write about/ discuss what happened to the failing company.

Notes

PRINCIPLE 54:
DON'T INVEST IN JUST A FEW STOCKS
(OR INVESTMENTS)

EXERCISE 44:

Write about/discuss the advantages and disadvantages of a diversified investment portfolio.

Notes

PRINCIPLES 56 AND 57:

EASY INVESTMENT MANAGEMENT AT A YOUNG AGE: PURCHASE THREE OR FOUR STOCK-INDEX MUTUAL FUNDS; ALWAYS BUY NO-LOAD RATHER THAN LOAD MUTUAL FUNDS

EXERCISE 45:

There are many types of mutual funds. List as many fund types as you can—which one interests you the most? Why?

Notes

PRINCIPLE 58:

INVEST IN YOUR 401(K)—AT LEAST TO YOUR COMPANY MATCH

EXERCISE 46:

There are two different types of 401(k)s—traditional and Roth. Explain the difference between the two.

Notes

PRINCIPLE 59:
DON'T INVEST WITH FAMILY AND FRIENDS (OR LOAN THEM MONEY)

EXERCISE 47:

Do you agree or disagree with this statement? Why? Write about/discus your thoughts.

Notes

Housing and Insurance Lessons

PRINCIPLES 60 AND 61:
RENTING—RENT DON'T BUY (UNTIL YOU'RE SETTLED); BUDGET 25 PERCENT OF YOUR GROSS SALARY

EXERCISE 48:

What are the advantages and disadvantages to renting? Owning? Which would you prefer? Write about/discuss your thoughts.

Notes

PRINCIPLE 62:

IF YOU HAVE PAID ONE MONTH'S SECURITY DEPOSIT, DON'T PAY YOUR LAST MONTH'S RENT

EXERCISE 49:

Is it ethical to follow this principle? Write about/discuss your thoughts.

Notes

PRINCIPLES 63, 64, AND 65:
BUYING A HOUSE

EXERCISE 50:

Everyone has his or her own preferences regarding what is important to him or her in a home. If you had the money to purchase a new home today, what would be the five most important factors to you? List and discuss them.

Notes

PRINCIPLES 66, 67, 68, AND 69:
MORTGAGE

EXERCISE 51:

Compare fifteen year fixed mortgage rates from three different companies (include one local bank). You can find many companies offering mortgages at bankrate. com and lendingtree.com (among others). Do the same with thirty year mortgages. Which company would you use, and why? Bonus exercise: besides fifteen and thirty year fixed mortgages, did you see any other types? And what benefits and risks did you see with them?

Notes

PRINCIPLES 70, 71, 72, AND 73:
INSURANCE

EXERCISE 52:

Interview someone who uses home, auto, health, and life insurance (or at least three of the four). Ask them to elaborate on the following: (1) How much does it cost? (2) Do they have high or low deductibles? (3) Are all the insurances they have necessities? (4) Have they ever had an insurance claim? and (5) What has been their experience with their insurance companies? Write a summary/discuss you interview.

Notes

Quick
Tips

PRINCIPLES 74–97:
TWENTY-FOUR QUICK TIPS

EXERCISE 53:

List your ranking of the top three quick tips in this section of the book. Elaborate on what you believe is the most important of these twenty-four quick tips. Bonus exercise: write about/discuss how you are going to incorporate the three tips into your life.

Notes

PRINCIPLE 98:

APPROACH YOUR JOB FOLLOWING THE THREE PS: PASSION, POLITENESS, AND PERSISTENCE

EXERCISE 54:

Which P do you believe is most important to your success at a job (you can identify your own P for this discussion)? Why? Write about/discuss your thoughts.

Notes

PRINCIPLE 99:
IT'S ALL UP TO YOU

EXERCISE 55:

Knowing that "it's all up to you," what are you going to (1) stop, (2) start, and (3) continue doing that will make you better at managing your money? Write about/discuss your thoughts.

Notes

AFTERWORD

Hopefully, this workbook was useful to you. My purpose for developing it was twofold. Firstly, to further improve the money-management skills of those individuals who read my book *Why Didn't They Teach Me This in School? 99 Personal Money Management Principles to Live By*. And secondly, to make it easier for professors, teachers, and parents to teach young adults the principles from my book. If I did that for you, then I succeeded in my endeavor.

If you have any questions or would like personalized/group training in personal money management, please contact me at carysiegel@yahoo.com, or visit my website, whydidnttheyteach methisinschool.com.

41529284R00077

Made in the USA
Lexington, KY
07 June 2019